Wild Flowers

The Wild Flowers of Britain and Northern Europe

Wild Flowers

The Wild Flowers of Britain and Northern Europe

Marjorie Blamey

Richard Fitter

Alastair Fitter

with a foreword by

Geoffrey Grigson

TIGER BOOKS INTERNATIONAL, LONDON

Originally published in 1974

© in this edition 1987 Marjorie Blamey,
Richard Fitter, Alastair Fitter

Designed by B. E. Rockett

Filmset by Jolly and Barber Ltd, Rugby

Reproduction by Adroit Photo Litho Ltd,
Birmingham

Made and printed in Great Britain by
Wm Collins Sons and Co Ltd, Glasgow

Contents

Foreword

The *Wild Flowers* of Britain and Northern Europe – has it occurred to you that we make a slight difficulty for ourselves in talking about plants as 'flowers'? Often the habit gets writers into trouble. Yet it is a wise, or poetic trick, to our credit. On the whole it is by their flowers that we first distinguish one species from another. Plants, at the right time, hold up their flower-faces, white, coloured, streaked, or spotted, and 'flowers' we call them. In 'flowers' – still attached to pedicels, stalks and leaves – we find our commonest lyricism, valid and comforting.

I do not know a modern flower-book – 'flower' again, you see – as concisely pleasing and efficient as this one, especially in its new enlarged form. It harmonizes – intellectual elements apart – with flowers as carnival and treasure-hunt. In the British Isles and northern Europe – certainly in the British Isles – we do have what is called an 'impoverished' flora. But that amounts to curtailment of the number of species rather than curtailment of the spectacle of flowers. The year comes round, primroses, then foxgloves, blossom down a Cornish cliff to the shag's nest and the sea almost, and on Yorkshire drumlins (rounded hillocks of glacial drift), orchids and Bistort in the grass parade all their pink spikes. No doubt of the yearly carnival.

Then, bad as 'impoverished' or 'impoverishment' may sound, it amounts as well to an expression of rarity; or in reverse, rarity goes with our impoverishment. For one reason or another, soil, climate, exposure, geological history, landscape history, human history, some plants are rare; and rarity introduces the lyricism of the treasure-hunt, of the find.

In many lives, over many centuries, thrilling moments have included the finding of some rare plant, at last; some plant – some flower I must say – known by plate and fame, encountered at last rooted firmly and happily into its natural home.

Pleasure derives, too, from local abundance, contrasting with scarcity or absence in some more familiar locality. Grow up in Cornwall (as I did), and you grow up with the best, biggest, softest, most freshly scented primroses; but you know nothing of cowslips. Grow up in Wiltshire, and you know cowslips as well as primroses; but nothing of oxlips – that requires a shift to Essex – and nothing of birdseye primrose, the little deliciously pink primula of the northern moors.

When – after that Cornish childhood – I was in the flush of discovering the northern limestone and becoming acquainted with Birdseye Primrose, I realized one day – suddenly – the significance (which no editor had spotted or recorded) of some lines in one of the most ecstatic English poems, Christopher Smart's *Song to David*:

> The grass the polyanthus cheques,
> And polish'd porphyry reflects,
> By the descending rill.

The polyanthus was Birdseye Primrose, the polish'd porphyry was the polished limestone of a little waterfall. Christopher Smart was remembering his childhood in Teesdale, in Co. Durham.

To the flower pleasures, then, of carnival and treasure-hunt must be added such human-historical pleasures.

Since the eighteenth century, the wild flowers of these islands have been so loved, so studied by professional and amateur field-botanists, that a delightful history could be written of the relationships of flowers and men. When I see the artificial, still unexplained Silbury Hill, part of the prehistoric complex of Avebury, I often remember how, in search of plants, Silbury was climbed, some time in mid-sixteenth century, by the Flemish botanist de l'Obel (eponym of the species *Lobelia*). On the way up or the way down, Matthias de l'Obel found Squinancywort, and recorded it, the first time the species had been recognized in Britain.

In the most curious ways flowers will thread our lives, flowers will lead to new experiences and tie them inextricably with the older experiences. When I lived in Cornwall, few flowers gave me more local patriotic pleasure than the minute Cornish moneywort, scrawling over damp rock. We know that as a 'British plant' it was first discovered – in Cornwall – by the great naturalist, John Ray, on July 1st, 1662, near St Ives. Its specific name *Sibthorpia* led me to facts about John Sibthorpe, Oxford botanist of the eighteenth century, led me to his memorial in Bath Abbey, a relief by Flaxman which shows Sibthorpe in ancient Greek costume, with a bunch of flowers in his hand, stepping ashore in Elysium or Greece (he compiled a huge *Flora Graeca*), led me to the journal of Sibthorpe's flower explorations in Cyprus, which in turn led me to decide I must go to Cyprus, and see one flower he described, *Hyoscyamus aureus*, Golden Henbane, a beauty with violet, almost black throated flowers of yellow. Sibthorpe said it grew on the old walls of Kyrenia; and there it was, there it was. After which – all because of a minute, obscure plant in a Cornish ditch – I went on to the other delights of Cyprus, floral and archaeological.

Yet all floral pleasures depend on recognition, on wild flower guides, on keys, and descriptions, and on the flowers pictured. As aid to identification, colour photos are inferior to paintings. They cannot point sharply to the finer, irrefutable characteristics. One of the least of Marjorie Blamey's watercolours shows this, in a way which happens to involve just one more experience of my own. Lately, in April, in falling, then melting snow, I looked for a mill in the north of France which was described in his reminiscences by the dramatist Ionesco. He had been farmed out there as a child. I found the mill, and beside the stream, on black, wet ground, below alders, were splashes, or clumps, of the most singing, startling purple flower I had ever seen. A toothwort, yes – that was obvious; in fact Purple Toothwort (*Lathraea clandestina*). But it could be identified at once from Mrs Blamey's watercolour (93), although she had found space only for a single blossom.

There is more than help in these plates. One after another the best of them concentrate that lyricism of flowers. I admire the sombre poetry of the green and yellow plates, or green and brown plates, the Willows (2, 3) and other catkin bearers (4, 5). I admire (seldom as well done) the white umbellifers (65) and the white crucifers (34, 35). But then look at those outbursts of organized colour, the knapweeds and star thistles (107), the irises, gladiolus, crocuses (119), the poppies (28), and the cranesbills (53). There you have the Earth Carnival, all right, the gaiety of the business.

GEOFFREY GRIGSON.

Introduction

The decision to issue *The Wild Flowers of Britain and Northern Europe* (first published in 1974) in a new, large format was prompted mainly by the immediate and enthusiastic reception given to the 126 plates painted for the book by Marjorie Blamey. In this larger format, these plates can now be seen to their best advantage. Furthermore, advances in techniques of colour reproduction since the original edition of the book have meant that the plates have gained considerably in clarity and accuracy. For these reasons alone, the book would serve as an admirable complement to any identification guide. But more than that, the plates do bring out, far better than those of the earlier volume, the sheer beauty and variety of our native flora.

The intentions of this book are thus different from those of its predecessor. It is hoped that the present volume will serve less as an identification guide, and more as an introduction to, and a reminder of, the pleasure to be had from a knowledge of wild flowers: and that it will familiarise people with rare and uncommon flowers that they might not otherwise notice in the countryside around them.

Some notes on the criteria used in the compilation of this book, and on the best way in which the book itself may be used, are given below.

Area Covered The area covered by this book lies roughly between Arctic Norway in the north and the river Loire in western and central France and the river Danube in Germany in the south. Its boundary runs along the Loire from its mouth on the Atlantic coast of France eastwards to Dijon and Basle and thence along the Danube and the foothills of the Alps to Munich, so as to include the Vosges and the Black Forest, but excluding the Jura and the Alps. At Munich it turns northwards across Germany through Regensburg, Bayreuth, Erfurt and Brunswick to reach the Baltic at Lübeck, and thence up the Gulf of Finland and the eastern frontier of Finland to the Arctic Ocean. Iceland is included. These boundaries are shown on the map on p. xi.

The Plates The plates have been grouped together in the first section of the book, rather than interleaved with the caption pages. The sequence follows that of *The Wild Flowers of Britain and Northern Europe*. Thus, with the exception of the flowering trees and tall shrubs, which are placed at the beginning for convenience, the order is in agreement with established taxonomic convention.

Each plant is labelled with its English common name. These names follow in most cases the list approved by the Botanical Society of the British Isles.

On each plate, there is a reference to the text page(s) on which the descriptions of the plants illustrated will be found.

Most of the plants are shown one-and-a-half times life size, but where there is any deviation from this rule, a single flower of the plant in question is also shown at one-and-a-half times life size. Only the Iris plate (Plate 119) is painted to the smaller scale of three-quarters life size. Where two or more plants resemble each other closely, only one of them has been shown in full: the remainder are illustrated simply with their distinguishing characteristics.

The Text The text in this edition, apart from some minor revisions, has been little altered from the text of *The Wild Flowers of Britain and Northern Europe*. There are fewer abbreviations and only those plants illustrated are actually described, each with a reference to the plate on which it occurs.

The species descriptions are arranged under family and generic headings, and group descriptions of families and genera are given wherever possible, so as to avoid constant repetition of common characters – for example, the shape of a pea flower or the nature of a composite flower. They should therefore always be read carefully and in conjunction with the species descriptions. The group descriptions refer only to species mentioned in the text.

Each text description includes standardised information, giving details that are largely confined to points such as height, flowering period, habitat, and distribution, which are either difficult to illustrate or which, by their very nature, cannot be illustrated at all. The major diagnostic features distinguishing the plant from other similar plants with which it might be confused, are shown in italics. A number of assumptions are made in the descriptions: unless otherwise stated, plants are erect and herbaceous, leaves are stalked, flowers are open.

Latin scientific names in general follow *Flora Europaea* (where available), otherwise as in Polunin's *A Field Guide to the Flowers of Europe* or Dandy's *List of British Vascular Plants*.

Plants native to Britain, or commonly naturalised in the British Isles, are preceded by an asterisk.

Height is indicated as follows:

Tall	Medium	Short	Low
over 60 cm (2 ft)	30–60 cm (1–2 ft)	10–30 cm (4–12 in)	0–10 cm (0–4 in)

Plant sizes can vary greatly according to altitude, climate and soil. Plants are more likely to be found smaller than is indicated here than larger.

Annual, biennial or perennial status is given in each case. Perennials are usually stouter than annuals, and of course are much more likely to be seen above ground in winter.

Leaf shapes and flower shapes and arrangements are also described. The terms used may in some cases be unfamiliar, but all are defined in the Glossary (page xiii). Flower sizes are diameters unless otherwise stated. Flower colour refers to petals or to sepals when there are no petals. It is more variable in some species than others. Most pink, mauve, purple and blue flowers produce white forms from time to time, and many white flowers can be tinged pink. Some, such as milkworts (Plate 55), are exceptionally variable. But a normally coloured flower is usually to be found nearby.

Flowering time refers to the central part of the area, and may be earlier in the south, near the sea and in forward seasons, and later in the north, on mountains and in backward seasons.

Fruits are usually only described where important for identification.

Habitats, such as fen and bog, are used here in their strict sense, see Glossary (page xiii). Areas with lime (chalk or limestone) in the soil are shown in the map opposite.

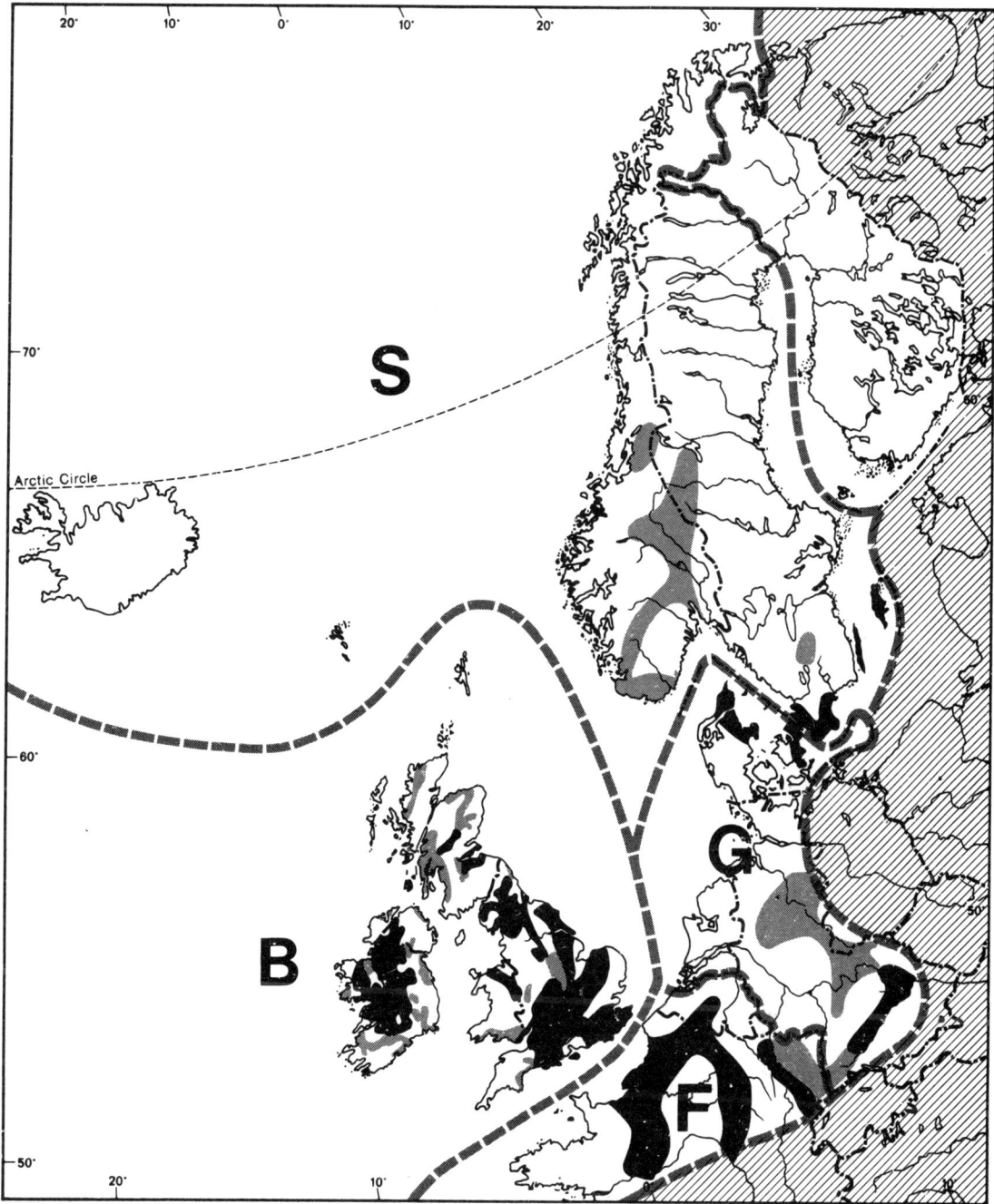

region not covered by this book

boundary between distribution areas

major outcrops of chalk and limestone

scattered outcrops of chalk and limestone

The following symbols show whether the plant occurs, either commonly or uncommonly, within each region. If it has only a very few localities, 'rare' is added, and if it is mainly found, e.g., in the south of the region, the word 'southern' is also added.

T – Throughout the area covered by the book (see above).

B – Great Britain, Ireland, Isle of Man.

F – France, Belgium, Luxembourg, Channel Islands.

G – Germany, the Netherlands, Denmark.

S – Norway, Sweden, Iceland, the Faroes.

If parentheses enclose the symbol – for example, (G) – the plant is introduced, not native. The great majority of introduced plants occur on waste or disturbed ground, roadsides, or other habitats much affected by human activity. Only rarely, as with New Zealand Willowherb (Plate 61), do they succeed in invading natural or semi-natural habitats, such as heaths, moors and calcareous grassland.

Abbreviations used in the Text

Sp.	Species (singular)
Spp.	Species (plural)
Ssp.	Subspecies
Var.	Variety
*	Native or commonly naturalised in Britain.
B, F, G, S,	Found in Britain, France, Germany, Scandinavia, and
and T.	Throughout respectively. See above.
( )	Indicates the plant is introduced, not native.

Glossary

Acid soils have very few basic minerals and are formed on rocks such as sandstone. Peaty soils are usually acid since plant humus is often so.

Alternate: neither opposite nor whorled.

Anther: the part of the flower producing the male pollen.

Annual plants live for a year or less. They are usually shallow rooted and never woody.

Appressed: flattened against the stem.

Berry: fleshy fruit.

Biennials: live for two years. Usually the first year's growth produces a leaf-rosette, the second the flowers.

Bog: a habitat on wet, acid peat.

Bracts are small, usually leaf-like organs just below the flowers, and sometimes, as in Daisies, numerous and overlapping.

Bulbs are underground storage organs, composed of fleshy leaves.

Bulbils are small bulb-like organs at the base of the leaves or in place of the flowers, breaking off to form new plants.

Calyx refers to the sepals as a whole, usually used when they are joined.

Casual: plant appearing irregularly, without fixed localities.

Catkins are hanging flower-spikes, the individual flowers of which are usually rather inconspicuous.

Cluster: loose group of flowers.

Composite: member of the Daisy Family, Compositae.

Corms are bulb-like underground storage organs, comprising a swollen stem.

Coppice: trees or shrubs cut to the ground and growing from the old stools.

Corolla refers to the petals as a whole, usually when they are joined.

Crucifer: member of Cabbage Family, Cruciferae.

Deciduous: with leaves falling in autumn.

Deflexed: bent downwards.

Dunes are areas of wind-blown, usually lime-rich shell sand near the sea, with intervening damp hollows, termed *slacks*.

Epicalyx is a ring of sepal-like organs just below the true sepals (calyx). Common in Rose Family.

Female flowers contain styles only, no stamens.

Fen: a habitat on wet, lime-rich peat, not acid as in a bog (q.v.).

Florets are small flowers, part of a compound head.

Flower: the reproductive structure of a plant.

Flower parts comprise petals, sepals, stamens, styles, and sometimes other organs.

Alternate

Anther

Appressed

Bracts

Bulbil

Calyx

Catkins

Cluster

Composite

Corolla

Fruits are composed of the seeds and structures surrounding them.

Head: used when flowers are grouped in more or less compact terminal groups.

Heath: area, often dominated by heathers or related shrubs, on acid soils.

Hips are usually brightly coloured false fruits, characteristic of roses.

Hoary: greyish with short hairs.

Honey-leaf; see Nectary.

Introduced plants are not native to the area, but brought in by man.

Labiate: belonging to the Labiate Family, Labiatae.

Lanceolate: spear-shaped, narrowly oval and pointed.

Lax: of a flower-head with the flowers well spaced; not dense.

Lime: strictly the product (Calcium oxide) of the burning of limestone rock (Calcium carbonate), but here used loosely to include limestone and chalk, and also soils formed on them; the opposite of acid. Lime-rich soils are those formed on limestone.

Linear: almost parallel-sided.

Lobed: of leaves deeply toothed, but not formed of separate leaflets; cf. pinnate.

Male flowers contain stamens only, no styles.

Marsh: a community on wet ground, but not on peat.

Microspecies: species produced by complex reproductive processes which result in a large number of biologically distinct units, only distinguished with difficulty, and often on microscopic characters.

Midrib: central vein of a leaf, usually thick and raised.

Moor: usually heather covered, upland areas.

Morphology: the study of the shape, form or appearance of plants.

Nectar: sugary substance attractive to insects and secreted by many flowers.

Nectary: organ in the flower producing nectar.

Net-veined: of a leaf with the veins not all parallel.

Node: point of origin of leaves on the stem.

Opposite: of leaves arising opposite each other on the stem.

Palmate: with finger-like lobes or leaflets.

Parasites: are plants, usually without green colouring, that obtain nutriment from other plants.

Peat is a soil composed of undecayed plant matter, often acid.

Perennial: plant surviving more than two years; often stouter than annuals and sometimes woody.

Petals: usually conspicuous organs above the sepals, and surrounding the reproductive parts of the flower.

Pinnate, Pinnatifid: see Figure.

Pod: fruit, usually long and cylindrical and never fleshy; as in peas.

Rhizome: horizontal underground stem, and therefore bearing leaf-scars.

Rosette: flattened, rose-like group of leaves at the base of the stem.

Deflexed

Disc florets

Epicalyx

Female flower

Lobed

Male flower

Midrib

Nectary

Net-veined

Nodes

Pinnate

Rhizome

Rosette

Runners are horizontal above-ground stems, often rooting at the nodes.

Samara: a winged key-shaped fruit.

Scale: small appendage not resembling a leaf. Normally small, brown, and papery.

Sepals form a ring immediately below the petals and are usually green or brown and less conspicuous.

Shrub: much-branched woody plant, shorter than a tree.

Shy flowerer: plant often passing whole years without flowering and for which other characters are therefore important for identification.

Species: the basic unit of classification.

Spike: flower-head with flowers arranged up a central axis in a cylinder. Stalked spike has individual flowers stalked.

Spine: straight, sharp-tipped appendage; cf. thorn.

Spreading: standing out horizontally or at a wide angle from the stem.

Stamens: the male organs in a flower, comprising a filament and a pollen sac, the anther (see Figure). Distinguished from styles (q.v.) by lying outside the centre of the flower usually in a ring, and by the usually coloured anthers.

Stigma: the surface receptive to pollen at the tip of the style.

Stipules are scale- or leaf-like organs at the base of the leaf-stalk.

Styles: the columns of filaments leading from the female organs to the stigma (q.v.); see Figure. Distinguished from stamens (q.v.) by lying in the centre of the flower, within the ring of stamens.

Subspecies: the division in the classification of organisms immediately below the species. Subspecies are morphologically distinct from each other, but interbreed freely and are therefore included in the same species.

Tendrils are twisted filaments forming part of a leaf or stem and used for climbing.

Thallus: plant body not differentiated into stems and leaves.

Thorn: sharp-tipped, woody appendage, straight or curved.

Tree: tall, woody plant, with a single woody stem at the base.

Trefoil, Trifoliate: with three leaflets.

Umbel: a flowerhead with the flowers in a spike but the lower branches longer so that all are level. **Umbellifers** are members of the Umbelliferae, characterised by having flowers in umbels.

Undershrub: low, often creeping woody perennial, often quite unlike taller shrubs.

Variety: a distinct form of a plant, of even lower rank than a subspecies.

Waste places: areas much disturbed by man, but not cultivated.

Whorl: where several organs arise at the same point on a stem; cf. opposite

Winged: with a flange running down the stem or stalk.

Wings: see page 26.

Runners

Samara

Scales

Sepals

Spike

Stamens

Stigma

Stipules

Style

Tendrils

Thorn

Whorl

Winged fruit

Winged stem

Winged flower

The Plates

PLATE 1
page 1

Silver
Fir

Douglas
Fir

Norway
Spruce

Western
Hemlock

Scots
Pine

European
Larch

Maritime
Pine

Joint
Pine

Lawson's
Cypress

Yew

Juniper

PLATE 2
pages 1–2

Bay
Willow

White
Willow

Crack
Willow

Grey
Willow

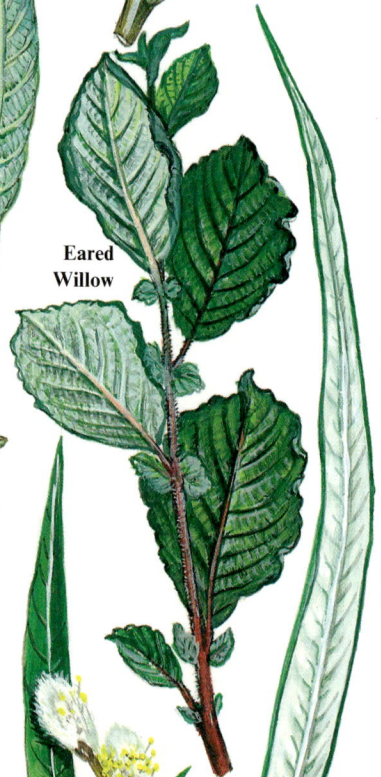

Goat
Willow

Eared
Willow

Purple
Willow

Violet
Willow

Osier

PLATE 3
page 2

Dark-leaved Willow

Downy Willow

Woolly Willow

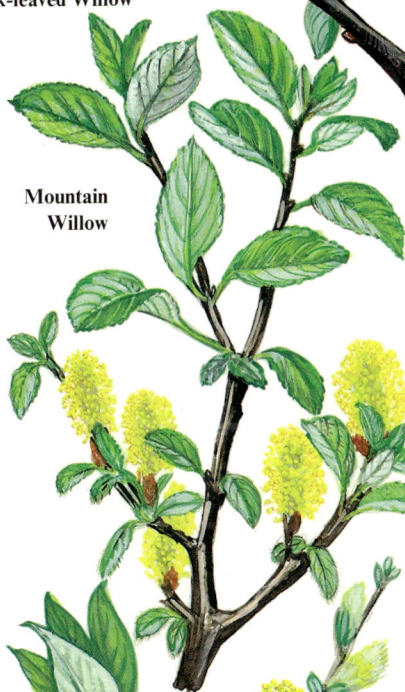

Mountain
Willow

Whortle-leaved
Willow

Spear-leaved
Willow

Net-
leaved
Willow

Creeping
Willow

Dwarf Willow

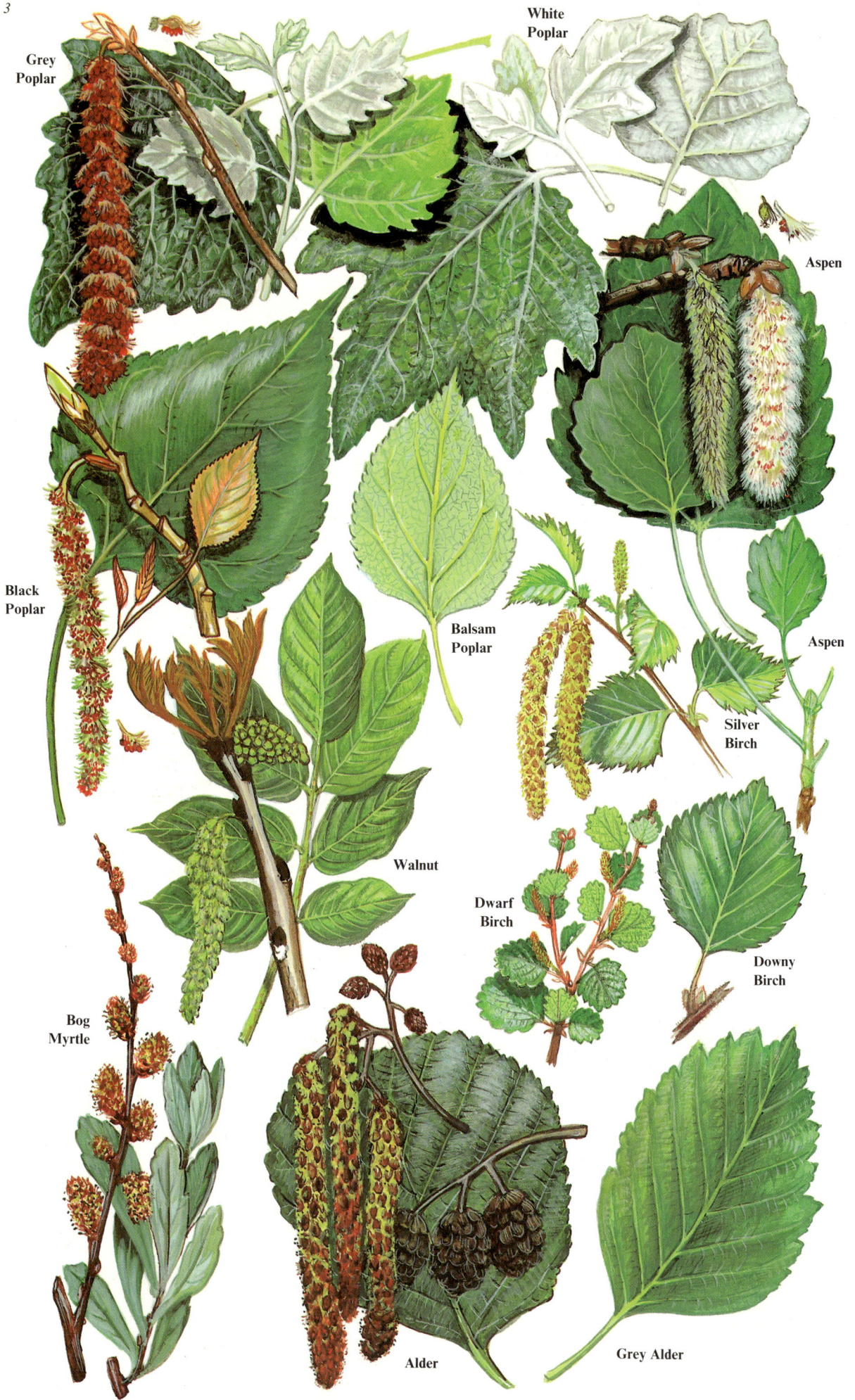

PLATE 4
page 3

Grey
Poplar

White
Poplar

Aspen

Black
Poplar

Balsam
Poplar

Aspen

Silver
Birch

Walnut

Dwarf
Birch

Downy
Birch

Bog
Myrtle

Alder

Grey Alder

PLATE 5
pages 3–4

Hornbeam

Hazel

Beech

Sweet
Chestnut

Evergreen
Oak

Sessile
Oak

Pedunculate
Oak

Turkey
Oak

Red Oak

PLATE 6
page 4

Wych Elm

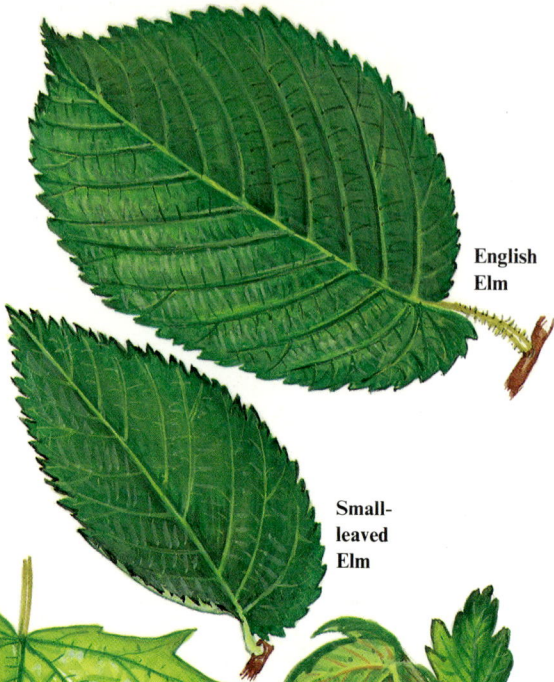

English Elm

Norway Maple

Small-leaved Elm

London Plane

Sycamore

Italian Maple

Field Maple

Montpelier Maple

PLATE 7
pages 4–5

Horse Chestnut

Holly

Small-leaved Lime

Large-leaved Lime

Ash

Tree of Heaven

PLATE 8
pages 5–6

Birthwort

Asarabacca

Mistletoe

Bastard
Toadflax

Hop

Pellitory
of
the
Wall

Hemp

Nettle

Annual Nettle

PLATE 9
page 6

Bistort

Amphibious
Bistort

Redshank

Pale
Persicaria

Alpine
Bistort

Water-
pepper

Sea Knotgrass

Buckwheat

Knotgrass

PLATE 10
pages 6–7

Copse
Bindweed

Black
Bindweed

Japanese
Knotweed

Himalayan
Knotweed

Iceland
Purslane

Hottentot
Fig

Spring
Beauty

Pink
Purslane

Blinks

PLATE 11

page 7

Common
Sorrel

Sheep's
Sorrel

Sheep's Sorrel

Clustered
Dock

Broad-
leaved
Dock

Marsh
Dock

Mountain
Sorrel

Fiddle
Dock

Water
Dock

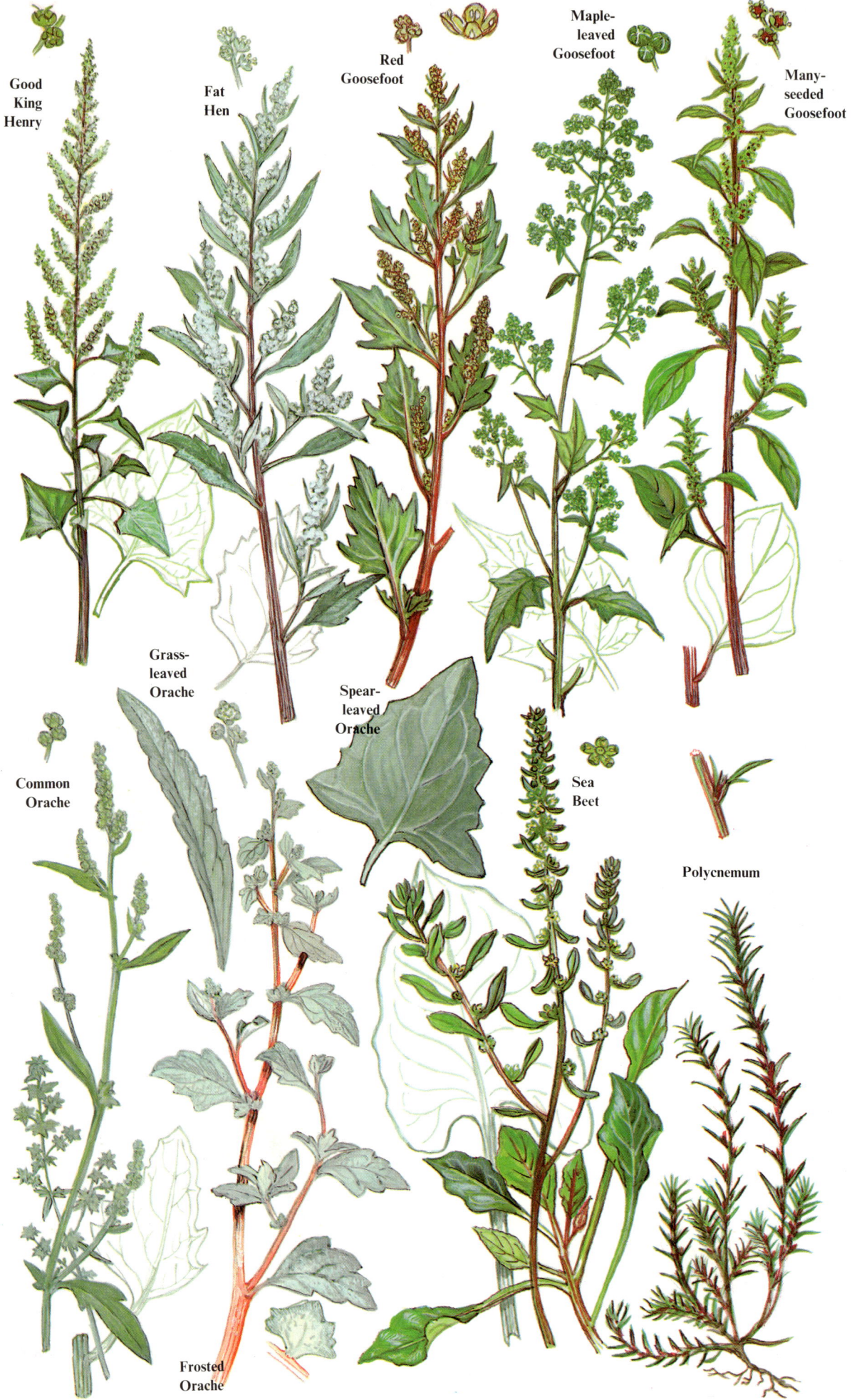

PLATE 12
page 8

Good
King
Henry

Fat
Hen

Red
Goosefoot

Maple-
leaved
Goosefoot

Many-
seeded
Goosefoot

Grass-
leaved
Orache

Spear-
leaved
Orache

Sea
Beet

Common
Orache

Polycnemum

Frosted
Orache

PLATE 13
page 8

Sea
Purslane

Glasswort

Annual
Seablite

Prickly
Saltwort

Shrubby
Seablite

Hairy
Seablite

Green
Amaranth

PLATE 14
page 9

Arctic
Sandwort

Three-
veined
Sandwort

Spring
Sandwort

Thyme-
leaved
Sandwort

Fine-
leaved
Sandwort

Curved
Sandwort

Sea
Sandwort

Cyphel

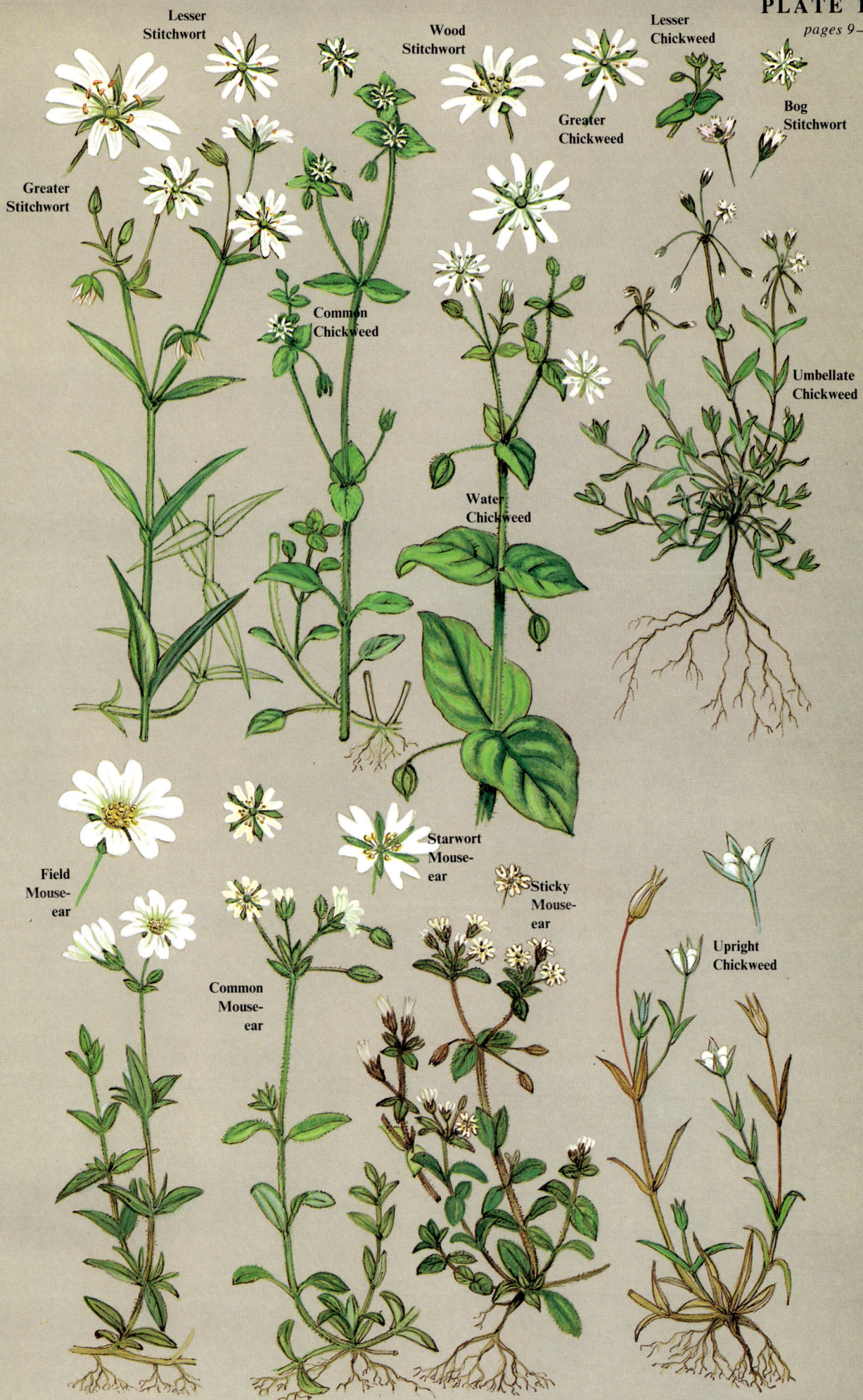

PLATE 15

pages 9–10

Lesser
Stitchwort

Wood
Stitchwort

Lesser
Chickweed

Greater
Chickweed

Bog
Stitchwort

Greater
Stitchwort

Common
Chickweed

Umbellate
Chickweed

Water
Chickweed

Field
Mouse-
ear

Starwort
Mouse-
ear

Sticky
Mouse-
ear

Upright
Chickweed

Common
Mouse-
ear

PLATE 16

page 10

Corn
Spurrey

Greater
Sea
Spurrey

Lesser
Sea
Spurrey

Heath
Pearlwort

Knotted
Pearlwort

Procumbent
Pearlwort

Annual
Knawel

Strapwort

Smooth
Rupturewort

Four-
leaved
Allseed

Coral
Necklace

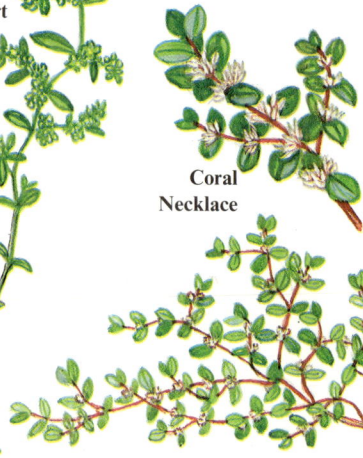

PLATE 17
pages 10–11

Nottingham
Catchfly

White
Sticky
Catchfly

Bladder
Campion

Spanish
Catchfly

Sea Campion

Moss
Campion

Flaxfield
Catchfly

Sweet
William
Catchfly

Northern
Catchfly

Rock
Catchfly

Forked
Catchfly

PLATE 18
page 11

Red Campion

White Campion

Night-flowering Catchfly

Ragged Robin

Sticky Catchfly

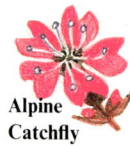

Alpine Catchfly

Corn Cockle

Soapwort

PLATE 19
pages 11–12

Small-flowered Catchfly

Sand Catchfly

Berry Catchfly

Fastigiate Gypsophila

Cow Basil

Tunic Flower

Proliferous Pink

Annual Gypsophila

PLATE 20
page 12

Cheddar
Pink

Wild
Pink

Clove
Pink

Jersey
Pink

Deptford
Pink

Carthusian
Pink

Maiden
Pink

Large
Pink

PLATE 21
pages 12–13

Stinking
Hellebore

Green
Hellebore

Love-in-
a-mist

Winter
Aconite

Yellow
Water-
lily

White
water-
lily

Least
Water-
lily

PLATE 22

page 13

Globe
Flower

Marsh Marigold

Meadow
Buttercup

Bulbous
Buttercup

Creeping
Buttercup

Greater
Spearwort

Lesser
Spearwort

Lesser Celandine

PLATE 23
pages 13–14

Celery-
leaved
Buttercup

Corn
Buttercup

Goldilocks
Buttercup

Small-
flowered
Buttercup

Large White
Buttercup

Glacier
Buttercup

Common
Water
Crowfoot

Ivy-
leaved
Crowfoot

PLATE 24
page 14

Common
Meadow-
rue

Greater
Meadow-
rue

Lesser
Meadow-
rue

Alpine
Meadow-rue

Baneberry

Traveller's
Joy

Alpine
Clematis

PLATE 25
pages 14–15

Columbine

Monkshood

Wolfsbane

Forking Larkspur

Varie-gated Monks-hood

Yellow Pheasant's-eye

Summer Pheasant's-eye

Large Pheasant's-eye

Mousetail

PLATE 26
page 15

Pale
Pasque
Flower

Eastern Pasque
Flower

Pasque
Flower

Wood
Anemone

Small
Pasque
Flower

Yellow
Anemone

Snowdrop
Windflower

Hepatica

PLATE 27
pages 15–16

Pale Corydalis

Barberry

Climbing Corydalis

Yellow Corydalis

Bulbous Corydalis

Ramping Fumitory

Small Fumitory

Common Fumitory

Oregon Grape

Wall Fumitory

PLATE 28
pages 16–17

Common
Poppy

Prickly
Poppy

Rough
Poppy

Long-
headed
Poppy

Opium
Poppy

Arctic
Poppy

Yellow-
Horned-
Poppy

Welsh Poppy

Greater
Celandine

PLATE 29
page 17

Yellow
Whitlow-
grass

Annual Wall
Rocket

Small Alison

Mountain Alison

Gold
of
Pleasure

Ball
Mustard

Buckler
Mustard

PLATE 30

pages 17–18

Wallflower

Hedge Mustard

Tall Rocket

Flixweed

Woad

Marsh Yellowcress

Common Wintercress

Creeping Yellowcress

Warty Cabbage

Treacle Mustard

Great Yellowcress

PLATE 31
page 18

Wild
Cabbage

Wild
Turnip

Black
Mustard

Charlock

Hairy
Rocket

Wallflower
Cabbage

Bastard
Cabbage

Wild
Radish

PLATE 32

pages 18–19

Narrow-
leaved
Bittercress

Cuckoo
Flower

Daisy-
leaved
Bittercress

Radish-
leaved
Bittercress

Large
Bittercress

Coralroot
Bittercress

Nine-
leaved
Bittercress

Garlic
Mustard

Dame's
Violet

Perennial
Honesty

Watercress

PLATE 33
page 19

Sea Kale

Sea
Rocket

Hoary
Stock

White
Ball
Mustard

Horse-
radish

Common
Scurvy-
grass

Early
Scurvy-
grass

Dittander

PLATE 34
pages 19–20

Tall Rockcress

Northern Rockcress

Hairy
Bittercress

Thale
Cress

Hairy
Rockcress

Tower
Mustard

Towercress

Alpine
Rockcress

Annual
Rockcress

PLATE 35
page 20

Wild Candytuft

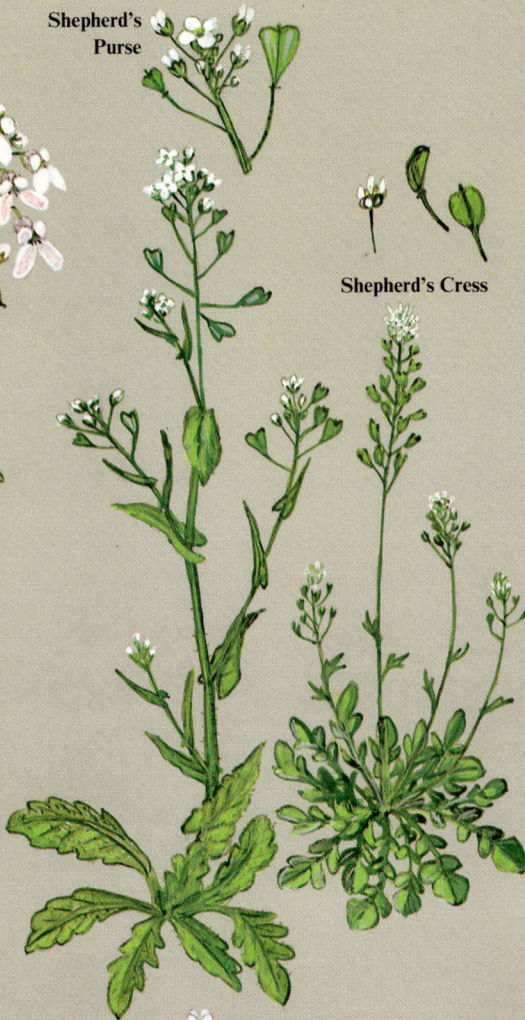

Shepherd's Purse

Shepherd's Cress

Hoary Alison

Sweet Alison

Wall Whitlow-grass

Common Whitlow-grass

Hutchinsia

PLATE 36

pages 20–21

Narrow-
leaved
Pepperwort

Hoary
Cress

Field
Pepperwort

Field
Pennycress

Garden
Cress

Swinecress

Alpine
Pennycress

Mountain
Pennycress

Perfoliate
Pennycress

Lesser
Swinecress

PLATE 37
pages 21–22

Weld

Wild
Mignonette

Great
Sundew

Oblong-
leaved
Sundew

Common
Sundew

Alternate-
leaved
Golden
Saxifrage

Grass of Parnassus

Opposite-
leaved
Golden
Saxifrage

Navelwort

Roseroot

PLATE 38
page 22

Orpine

Caucasian
Stonecrop

Biting
Stonecrop

White
Stonecrop

Reflexed
Stonecrop

Alpine
Stonecrop

Hen-
and-
chickens
Houseleek

Annual
Stonecrop

English
Stonecrop

Hairy
Stonecrop

Mossy Stonecrop

PLATE 39

pages 22–23

Starry
Saxifrage

St
Patrick's
Cabbage

Arctic
Saxifrage

Rue-
leaved
Saxifrage

Yellow
Saxifrage

Mossy
Saxifrage

Livelong
Saxifrage

Highland
Saxifrage

Hawkweed
Saxifrage

Meadow
Saxifrage

Purple
Saxifrage

PLATE 40
page 23

Meadowsweet

Goatsbeard
Spiraea

Great
Burnet

Salad
Burnet

Alpine
Lady's
Mantle

Agrimony

Lady's
Mantle

Parsley
Piert

PLATE 41
pages 23–24

Burnet
Rose

Dog
Rose

Field
Rose

Downy
Rose

Stone
Bramble

Cloudberry

Arctic
Bramble

Bramble

Raspberry

PLATE 42
pages 24–25

**Wild
Strawberry**

**Hautbois
Strawberry**

**Rock
Cinquefoil**

**Marsh
Cinquefoil**

Barren Strawberry

**Water
Avens**

Herb Bennet

**Mountain
Avens**

PLATE 43
page 25

Shrubby
Cinquefoil

Creeping
Cinquefoil

Trailing
Tormentil

Snow Cinquefoil

Tormentil

Hoary
Cinquefoil

Spring
Cinquefoil

Sulphur
Cinquefoil

Grey
Cinquefoil

Silverweed

Sibbaldia

PLATE 44
pages 25–26

Whitebeam

Hawthorn

Crab
Apple

Wild
Pear

Wild
Cherry

Bird
Cherry

Blackthorn

Amelanchier

Wild
Cherry

Wild
Cotoneaster

Small-
leaved
Cotoneaster

PLATE 45
page 26

Alpine
Milk-vetch

Purple
Milk-
vetch

Wild
Lentil

Yellow
Alpine
Milk-vetch

Wild
Liquorice

Goat's
Rue

Mountain
Milk-vetch

Crown
Vetch

Yellow
Milk-vetch

PLATE 46
pages 26–27

Western
Gorse

Dyer's
Greenweed

Laburnum

Gorse

Petty
Whin

Broom

Bladder
Senna

False
Acacia

Scorpion
Senna

Wild
Lupin

Tree
Lupin

PLATE 47
pages 27–28

Fodder Vetch

Tufted Vetch

Bush
Vetch

Upright
Vetch

Wood
Vetch

Spring
Vetch

Slender
Tare

Smooth
Tare

Bithynian
Vetch

Hairy
Tare

Yellow
Vetch

Common Vetch

PLATE 48
page 28

Meadow
Vetchling

Spring
Pea

Bitter
Vetchling

Sea
Pea

Broad-
leaved
Everlasting
Pea

Narrow-
leaved
Everlasting
Pea

Marsh
Pea

Tuberous
Pea

Hairy
Vetchling

Yellow
Vetchling

Grass
Vetchling

PLATE 49
pages 28–29

Sainfoin

Spiny
Rest-harrow

Large
Yellow
Rest-
harrow

Kidney Vetch

Rest-
harrow

Small Rest-harrow

Ribbed
Melilot

White
Melilot

Classical Fenugreek

Lucerne

ssp.
falcata

PLATE 50
page 29

Hairy
Birdsfoot
Trefoil

Horseshoe
Vetch

Dragon's
Teeth

Birdsfoot
Trefoil

Orange
Birdsfoot

Slender
Trefoil

Narrow-
leaved
Birdsfoot
Trefoil

Lesser
Trefoil

Birdsfoot

Spotted
Medick

Hop
Trefoil

Black
Medick

PLATE 51
pages 29–30

Sulphur
Clover

Alsike
Clover

Red
Clover

Mountain
Clover

White
Clover

Strawberry
Clover

Upright
Clover

Burrowing
Clover

Crimson
Clover

Suffocated
Clover

Haresfoot
Clover

Knotted
Clover

Fenugreek

PLATE 52

pages 30–31

Wood-
sorrel

Yellow
Oxalis

Pink Oxalis

Bermuda
Buttercup

Pale Flax

Common
Flax

Perennial
Flax

Yellow
Flax

Purging
Flax

Common
Storksbill

Sea Storksbill

Allseed

PLATE 53

page 31

Wood Cranesbill

Pencilled Cranesbill

Dusky
Cranesbill

Meadow
Cranesbill

French
Cranesbill

Marsh
Cranesbill

Bohemian
Cranesbill

Bloody
Cranesbill

Small-
flowered
Cranesbill

Little
Robin

Long-
stalked
Cranesbill

Hedgerow
Cranesbill

Herb
Robert

Shining
Cranesbill

Dovesfoot Cranesbill

Cut-
leaved
Cranesbill

PLATE 54

page 32

Wood
Spurge

Cypress
Spurge

Irish
Spurge

Sea
Spurge

Portland
Spurge

Caper
Spurge

Sun
Spurge

Petty
Spurge

Dwarf Spurge

Broad-
leaved
Spurge

Dog's
Mercury

Purple Spurge

PLATE 55
pages 32–33

Himalayan
Balsam

Touch-
me-
not
Balsam

Small
Balsam

Orange
Balsam

Burning
Bush

Spurge
Laurel

Annual
Thymelaea

Shrubby
Milkwort

Common
Milkwort

Heath Milkwort

Mezereon

PLATE 56

pages 33–34

Red
Currant

Black
Currant

Mountain
Currant

Gooseberry

Box

Buckthorn

Spindle-
tree

Bladder-
nut

Alder
Buckthorn

Sea
Buckthorn

Tamarisk

PLATE 57
page 34

Dwarf Mallow

Musk
Mallow

Least
Mallow

Common
Mallow

Tree
Mallow

Smaller
Tree
Mallow

Marsh
Mallow

Rough
Mallow

PLATE 58
pages 34–35

Tutsan

Rose of Sharon

Hairy St John's Wort

Perforate St John's Wort

Squarestalked St John's Wort

Slender St John's Wort

Trailing St John's Wort

Irish St John's Wort

Marsh St John's Wort

PLATE 59
pages 35–36

Early
Dog
Violet

Meadow
Violet

Pale
Dog
Violet

Sweet Violet

Common
Dog
Violet

Northern
Violet

Heath
Dog
Violet

Mountain
Pansy

Marsh Violet

Field
Pansy

Yellow
Wood
Violet

Wild
Pansy

Dwarf
Pansy

PLATE 60
page 36

White
Rock-
rose

Hoary
Rock-
rose

Common
Fumana

Sea-
heath

Common
Rock-
rose

Spotted
Rock-
rose

Large-
flowered
Evening
Primrose

White
Bryony

Enchanter's
Nightshade

Fragrant Evening Primrose

PLATE 61
pages 36–37

American
Willowherb

Hoary
Willowherb

Pale
Willowherb

Marsh
Willowherb

Square-
stemmed
Willowherb

Purple
Loosestrife

Broad-
leaved
Willowherb

Grass Poly

Great
Willowherb

Rosebay
Willowherb

New Zealand
Willowherb

Alpine Willowherb

PLATE 62
pages 37–38

Dogwood

**Dwarf
Cornel**

Ivy

**Cornelian
Cherry**

Sanicle

Astrantia

**Sea
Holly**

**Marsh
Pennywort**

**Field
Eryngo**

PLATE 63
page 38

Cow Parsley

Sweet Cicely

Bur Chervil

Upright Hedge Parsley

Knotted Bur Parsley

Rough Chervil

Caraway

Greater Bur Parsley

Coriander

Whorled Caraway

Wild Carrot

PLATE 64

pages 38–39

Pignut

Burnet
Saxifrage

Shepherd's
Needle

Ground
Elder

Moon Carrot

Spignel

Bladderseed

Honewort

Fool's
Parsley

PLATE 65
page 39

Hogweed

Angelica

Hemlock Water Dropwort

Hemlock

Greater Water-parsnip

Cowbane

Cambridge Milk-parsley

Pleurospermum

Longleaf

PLATE 66
pages 39–40

Fool's
Watercress

Wild
Celery

Tubular
Water
Dropwort

Lesser
Water-
parsnip

Parsley
Water
Dropwort

Fine-
leaved
Water
Dropwort

Stone
Parsley

Corn
Parsley

PLATE 67
page 40

Hog's
Fennel

Milk Parsley

Masterwort

Hartwort

Sermountain

Slender
Hare's-
ear

Cnidium

Scots
Lovage

PLATE 68
pages 40–41

Wild Parsnip

Alexanders

Rock Samphire

Fennel

Pepper Saxifrage

Lovage

Thorow-wax

Small Hare's-ear

Sickle Hare's-ear

PLATE 69
page 41

One-
flowered
Wintergreen

Intermediate
Wintergreen

Toothed
Wintergreen

Common
Wintergreen

Round-
leaved
Wintergreen

Yellow
Wintergreen

Norwegian
Wintergreen

Umbellate
Wintergreen

Yellow
Birdsnest

Diapensia

PLATE 70
pages 41–42

Heather

Bell
Heather

Dorset
Heath

Cross-
leaved
Heath

Cornish
Heath

Arctic
Rhododendron

Bog
Rosemary

Irish
Heath

Mountain
Heath

St
Dabeoc's
Heath

PLATE 71
page 42

Bilberry

Northern
Bilberry

Labrador Tea

Cowberry

Alpine
Bearberry

Cranberry

Leatherleaf

Cassiope

Wild
Azalea

Crowberry

Strawberry
Tree

PLATE 72
page 43

False
Oxlip

Oxlip

Birdseye
Primrose

Primrose

Cowslip

Scottish
Primrose

Yellow
Loosestrife

Alpine
Snowbell

Yellow
Pimpernel

Tufted
Loosestrife

Creeping
Jenny

PLATE 73
pages 43–44

Cyclamen

Chickweed
Wintergreen

Brookweed

Water Violet

Sowbread

Chaffweed

Northern
Androsace

Scarlet
Pimpernel

Sea
Milkwort

Blue
Pimpernel

Bog Pimpernel

PLATE 74

page 44

Thrift

Common
Sea-
lavender

Matted
Sea-
lavender

Rock
Sea-
lavender

Wild
Privet

Bogbean

Fringed
Water-
lily

Greater
Periwinkle

Vincetoxicum

Lesser
Periwinkle

PLATE 75
page 45

Perennial
Centaury

Common
Centaury

Yellow-wort

Lesser
Centaury

Great
Yellow
Gentian

Northern
Gentian

Yellow
Centaury

Guernsey
Centaury

PLATE 76
pages 45 –46

Marsh
Gentian

Purple
Gentian

Spring
Gentian

Cross
Gentian

Alpine
Gentian

Chiltern
Gentian

Autumn
Gentian

Field
Gentian

Marsh
Felwort

Slender
Gentian

Fringed
Gentian

PLATE 77
page 46

Hedge
Bindweed

Great
Bindweed

Jacob's
Ladder

Sea
Bindweed

Field
Bindweed

Field
Madder

Woodruff

Blue
Woodruff

Common
Dodder

Squinancywort

PLATE 78
pages 46–47

Hedge Bedstraw

Northern
Bedstraw

Crosswort

Wild
Madder

Lady's
Bedstraw

Heath
Bedstraw

Marsh
Bedstraw

Common
Cleavers

PLATE 79
page 47

Russian
Comfrey

Common
Comfrey

Yellow
Alkanet

Amsinckia

Houndstongue

Nonea

Corn
Gromwell

Purple
Gromwell

Common
Gromwell

PLATE 80
pages 47–48

Lungwort

Blue-
eyed
Mary

Wood
Forgetmenot

Field
Forgetmenot

Creeping
Forgetmenot

Water
Forgetmenot

Tufted
Forgetmenot

Jersey
Forgetmenot

Madwort

Changing
Forgetmenot

Bur
Forgetmenot

PLATE 81
page 48

Viper's
Bugloss

Green
Alkanet

Borage

Alkanet

Bugloss

Oyster
Plant

Vervain

PLATE 82

page 49

Bugle

Ground-
pine

Skullcap

Spear-
leaved
Skullcap

Lesser
Skullcap

Wood
Sage

Wall
Germander

Water
Germander

Cut-
leaved
Germander

Mountain
Germander

PLATE 83
pages 49–50

Self-
heal

Large
Self-heal

Ground
Ivy

White
Horehound

Catmint

Cut-
leaved
Self-
heal

Hairless
Catmint

Black
Horehound

Hyssop

Bastard
Balm

Winter
Savory

PLATE 84
page 50

Spotted
Dead-
nettle

Motherwort

Cut-
leaved
Dead-
nettle

Henbit
Dead-
nettle

White
Dead-nettle

Red
Dead-
nettle

Yellow
Archangel

Common
Hemp-
nettle

Red
Hemp-
nettle

Large-
flowered
Hemp-
nettle

Downy
Hemp-
nettle

PLATE 85
pages 50–51

Meadow
Clary

Wild
Sage

Wild
Clary

Balm

Limestone
Woundwort

Hedge
Woundwort

Marsh
Wound-
wort

Betony

Downy
Woundwort

Yellow
Woundwort

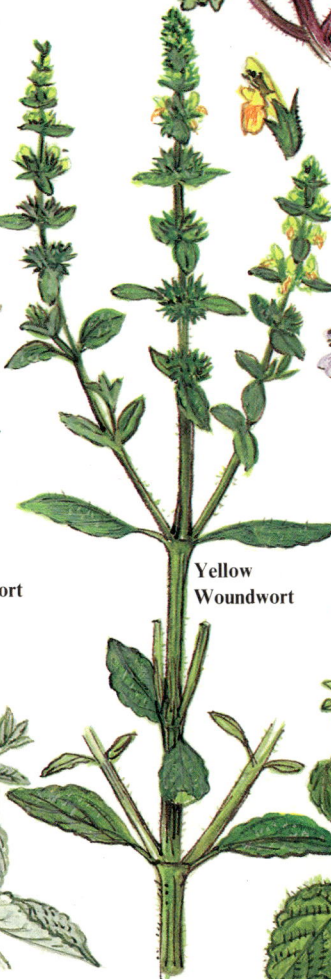

Field
Woundwort

PLATE 86
pages 51–52

Penny-
royal

Gipsywort

Corn
Mint

Water
Mint

Spear
Mint

Common Calamint

Basil
Thyme

Wild
Basil

Marjoram

Wild
Thyme

PLATE 87
page 52

Bittersweet

Black
Nightshade

Hairy
Nightshade

Deadly
Nightshade

Henbane

Small
Tobacco
Plant

Apple
of
Peru

Thorn-
apple

PLATE 88
pages 52–53

Great
Mullein

Dark Mullein

White
Mullein

Moth
Mullein

French
Figwort

Yellow
Figwort

Balm-leaved
Figwort

Common
Figwort

Large
Mullein

Purple
Mullein

PLATE 89
pages 53–54

Snapdragon

Common Toadflax

Sand Toadflax

Lesser Snapdragon

Daisy-leaved Toadflax

Jersey Toadflax

Alpine Toadflax

Round-leaved Fluellen

Field Toadflax

Pale Toadflax

Purple Toadflax

Ivy-leaved Toadflax

Small Toadflax

Sharp-leaved Fluellen

PLATE 90
page 54

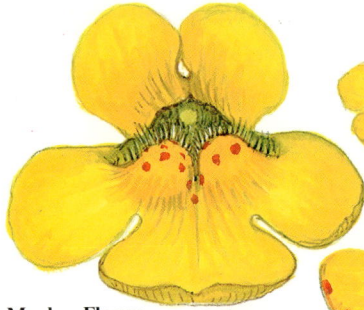

Monkey Flower

Musk

Blood-drop Emlets

Foxglove

Small Yellow Foxglove

Large Yellow Foxglove

Gratiola

Red Bartsia

Fairy Foxglove

Yellow Bartsia

Yellow Odontites

Alpine Bartsia

PLATE 91
pages 54–55

Spiked
Speedwell

Germander
Speedwell

Large
Speedwell

Common
Field
Speedwell

Ivy-
leaved
Speedwell

Brooklime

Water
Speedwell

Heath
Speedwell

Wall
Speedwell

Thyme-
leaved
Speedwell

Wood
Speedwell

Green
Field
Speedwell

Smooth
Speedwell

Grey
Field
Speedwell

Slender
Speedwell

Alpine
Speedwell

humifusa

Rock
Speedwell

Pink
Water
Speedwell

PLATE 92
pages 55–56

Yellow
Rattle

Lousewort

Marsh
Lousewort

Moor-
king

Eyebright

Field
Cow-
wheat

Small
Cow-
wheat

Crested
Cow-
wheat

Common
Cow-wheat

Leafy
Lousewort

Cornish
Moneywort

Wood Cow-wheat

PLATE 93
pages 56–57

Purple
Toothwort

Toothwort

Greater
Broomrape

Common
Broomrape

Purple
Broomrape

Large-
flowered
Butterwort

Globularia

Common
Butterwort

Clove-
scented
Broomrape

Pale
Butterwort

PLATE 94
page 57

Hoary
Plantain

Sea
Plantain

Branched
Plantain

Greater
Plantain

Ribwort
Plantain

Rannoch
Rush

Marsh
Arrow-
grass

Sea
Arrow-
grass

Moschatel

Buckshorn
Plantain

PLATE 95
pages 57–58

Marsh
Valerian

Red
Valerian

Cornsalad

Common
Valerian

Twinflower

Dwarf
Elder

Wayfaring
Tree

Honeysuckle

Guelder
Rose

Fly Honeysuckle

PLATE 96
pages 58–59

Field
Scabious

Yellow
Scabious

Grey
Scabious

Small
Scabious

Devilsbit
Scabious

Small
Teasel

Round-
headed
Rampion

Teasel

Spiked
Rampion

Sheepsbit
Scabious

PLATE 97

page 59

Harebell

Nettle-
leaved
Bellflower

Spreading
Bellflower

Clustered
Bellflower

Large
Venus's
Looking
Glass

Peach-
leaved
Bellflower

Bearded
Bellflower

Heath
Lobelia

Venus's
Looking
Glass

Ivy-leaved
Bellflower

PLATE 98
pages 59–60

Hemp
Agrimony

Goldilocks

Canadian
Fleabane

Golden-
rod

Canadian
Golden-
rod

Ploughman's
Spikenard

Golden
Samphire

Ragweed

Spiny
Cocklebur

PLATE 99
pages 60–61

Sea
Aster

Pineapple
Mayweed

Daisy

Scentless
Mayweed

Blue Fleabane

Shaggy
Soldier

Michaelmas
Daisy

Alpine
Fleabane

PLATE 100
page 61

Common
Cudweed

Mountain
Everlasting

Small
Cudweed

Marsh
Cudweed

Jersey
Cudweed

Heath
Cudweed

Helichrysum

Micropus

Small
Fleabane

PLATE 101
pages 61–62

Common
Fleabane

Irish
Fleabane

Yellow
Ox-
eye

Cone
Flower

Elecampane

Perennial
Sunflower

Arnica

Yellow Chamomile

Leopardsbane

PLATE 102
page 62

Butterbur

Winter
Heliotrope

Yarrow

Sneezewort

Mugwort

Trifid
Bur
Marigold

Sea
Wormwood

Cottonweed

Buttonweed

PLATE 103
pages 62–63

Ox-
eye
Daisy

Corn
Marigold

Feverfew

Tansy

Coltsfoot

Purple
Coltsfoot

Garden
Marigold

PLATE 104
page 63

Fen
Ragwort

Ragwort

Oxford
Ragwort

Marsh
Fleawort

Alpine
Ragwort

Silver
Ragwort

Field
Fleawort

Groundsel

PLATE 105
pages 63–64

Globe Thistle

Carline
Thistle

Alpine
Sawwort

Lesser
Burdock

Milk
Thistle

Stemless
Carline Thistle

Cabbage
Thistle

Cotton Thistle

PLATE 106
page 64

Woolly
Thistle

Spear
Thistle

Meadow
Thistle

Creeping
Thistle

Dwarf
Thistle

Musk
Thistle

Welted
Thistle

Slender
Thistle

Great
Marsh
Thistle

PLATE 107
pages 64–65

Black
Knapweed

Greater
Knapweed

Black
Knapweed

Cornflower

Perennial
Cornflower

Yellow
Star-
thistle

Red
Star-thistle

Sawwort

PLATE 108
page 65

Goatsbeard

Salsify

Purple
Viper's
Grass

Viper's
Grass

Purple
Lettuce

Chicory

Alpine
Sow-
thistle

Blue
Lettuce

PLATE 109
pages 65–66

Wall
Lettuce

Marsh
Sow-
thistle

Smooth
Sow-
thistle

Perennial
Sow-
thistle

Least
Lettuce

Nipplewort

Lamb's
Succory

Chondrilla

Prickly
Lettuce

PLATE 110
page 66

Dandelion

Red-
veined
Dandelion

Lesser
Dandelion

Common
Catsear

Rough
Hawkbit

Smooth
Catsear

Lesser
Hawkbit

Smooth
Hawksbeard

Mouse-
ear
Hawkweed

Spotted Catsear

PLATE 111

page 67

Leafy
Hawkweed

Hawkweed
Ox-
tongue

Bristly
Ox-
tongue

Few-
leaved
Hawkweed

Alpine
Hawkweed

Orange
Hawkweed

Northern
Hawksbeard

Marsh
Hawksbeard

Beaked
Hawksbeard

Rough Hawksbeard

PLATE 112
pages 67–68

Common
Water-
plaintain

Lesser
Water-
plantain

Floating
Water-
plantain

Star-fruit

Flowering
Rush

Parnassus-
leaved
Water-
plantain

Arrowhead

Water
Soldier

Frogbit